Big Machines in the Air

by Brienna Rossiter

FOCUS READERS®

SCOUT

www.focusreaders.com

Focus Readers is distributed by North Star Editions:
sales@northstareditions.com | 888-417-0195

Produced for Focus Readers by Red Line Editorial.

Photographs ©: Shutterstock Images, cover, 1, 4–5, 7 (top), 7 (bottom), 9 (top), 9 (bottom), 10–11, 12–13, 15, 16 (top left), 16 (top right), 16 (bottom left), 16 (bottom right)

Library of Congress Cataloging-in-Publication Data
Names: Rossiter, Brienna, author.
Title: Big machines in the air / by Brienna Rossiter.
Description: Lake Elmo, MN : Focus Readers, [2021] | Series: Big machines | Includes index. | Audience: Grades K-1.
Identifiers: LCCN 2020033507 (print) | LCCN 2020033508 (ebook) | ISBN 9781644936719 (hardcover) | ISBN 9781644937075 (paperback) | ISBN 9781644937792 (ebook pdf) | ISBN 9781644937433 (hosted ebook)
Subjects: LCSH: Flying-machines--Juvenile literature.
Classification: LCC TL547 .R635 2021 (print) | LCC TL547 (ebook) | DDC 629.133--dc23
LC record available at https://lccn.loc.gov/2020033507
LC ebook record available at https://lccn.loc.gov/2020033508

Printed in the United States of America
Mankato, MN
012021

About the Author

Brienna Rossiter is a writer and editor who lives in Minnesota. She loves being outside and traveling in airplanes.

Table of Contents

engine

Jet Planes

A jet takes off.

It has big **engines**.

It flies high above the ground.

Some jets carry people.

The people sit in rows.

Their bags go below.

bag

Some jets carry **cargo**.

They have large doors.

Boxes go inside.

cargo

Drones

Some people fly drones.

Drones do not have

people inside.

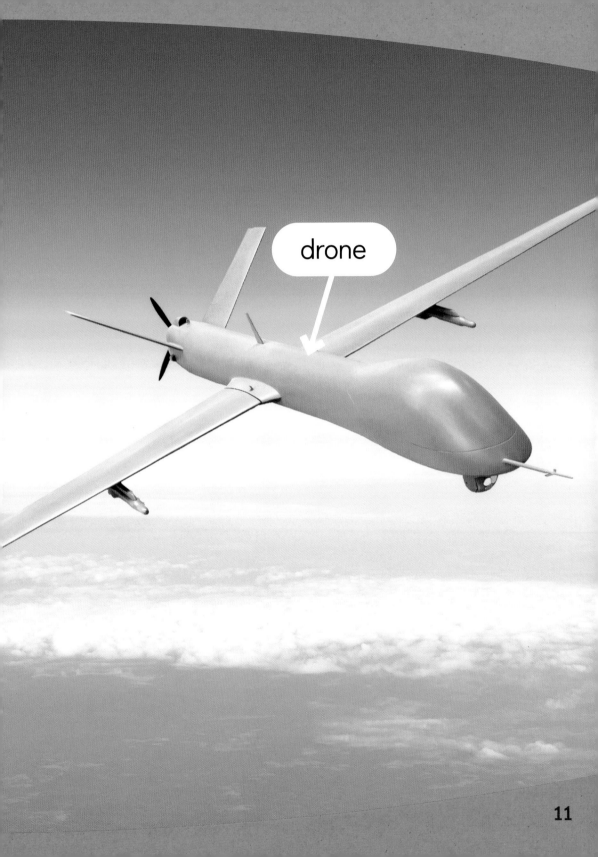

Other Ways to Fly

Gliders do not have engines.

They have long wings.

They glide through the air.

Helicopters have **rotors**.

The rotors spin fast.

Glossary

cargo

gliders

engines

rotors

Index